Avalanches

Avalanches

Patrick Merrick

THE CHILD'S WORLD®, INC.

Library of Congress Cataloging-in-Publication Data
Merrick, Patrick.
Avalanches/by Patrick Merrick.
p. cm.
Includes index.
Summary: Discusses, in question and answer format, what avalanches are, how they occur,
and how to protect oneself from avalanches.
ISBN 1-56766-414-8
1. Avalanches—Miscellanea—Juvenile literature.
[1. Avalanches—Miscellanea. 2. Questions and answers] I. Title.
QC929.A8M47 1997
551.3'07—dc21   97-11260
CIP
AC

Photo Credits

Brett Baunton/Tony Stone Images: 30
Cindy Jones/DEMBINSKY PHOTO ASSOC: cover, 9
COMSTOCK/COMSTOCK, Inc.: 19
COMSTOCK/R. Michael Stuckey: 29
DPA/DEMBINSKY PHOTO ASSOC: 24
Gary C. Baker/DEMBINSKY PHOTO ASSOC: 2
Gary Brettnacher/Tony Stone Images: 10
James Balog/Tony Stone Images: 16
Patrick Cone: 13, 15, 20, 23, 26
Rob Stapleton/DEMBINSKY PHOTO ASSOC: 6

On the cover...

Front cover: An avalanche at Liskim Ridge, Switzerland makes a cloud of snow.

Page 2: An avalanche in Colorado covers some trees.

Table of Contents

High in the mountains, clouds cover the sky. The steep slopes are covered in deep snow, and soon more begins to fall. All of the countryside is quiet and calm—but there is danger. Suddenly, a large amount of snow breaks loose from the mountain. A white wall of snow and ice rumbles down the slope. Everything in its path is buried. An avalanche is born!

Avalanches like this one make clouds of snow.

Where Do Avalanches Happen?

Avalanches can happen anywhere there are mountains or steep hills. In the United States, the Rocky Mountains have most of the avalanches. Other countries that have a lot of avalanches are Peru, Canada, China, Austria, and Switzerland. And one area in France has over 500 avalanches every year!

Alaskan mountains like this one also have a lot of avalanches.

How Do Avalanches Start?

It is hard to imagine how snow can be dangerous. To understand how avalanches work, you must learn about the snow itself. Snow is made up of tiny crystals. As the snow falls throughout the winter, the crystals pile on top of each other like the layers of a sandwich. With each snow storm, the layers keep growing and growing. In the mountains, some snow piles can be as much as 40 feet thick!

This snowy mountain in Canada is a perfect place for an avalanche.

With all this snow sitting on the side of a steep mountain, the layers can slide over each other and come tumbling down the mountain. This is an avalanche! To start the snow layers sliding, all it takes is a **vibration**, or small movement. Even sounds such as the voices of people or faraway trains can start an avalanche.

This avalanche in Utah started from a vibration.

Are There Different Types of Avalanches?

Since there are different types of snow, there are different types of avalanches. One type of avalanche is called a **dry snow avalanche**. In a dry snow avalanche, the snow is like a fine powder. As one snow crystal hits another, they start sliding down the hill. Soon the whole mountain of powder comes rumbling down. A dry snow avalanche can reach speeds of 200 miles per hour!

This dry snow avalanche is moving quickly down a mountain .

Another type of avalanche is called the **slab avalanche**. In this type, the snow is packed very tight. With the smallest vibration, huge chunks of snow begin sliding down the mountain. On February 5, 1983, a chunk of snow that was 30 feet thick started an avalanche in Alaska. When the avalanche was over, the valley below the mountain had enough snow in it to fill 22 football fields!

These people are digging out from a snowy avalanche.

How Dangerous Are Avalanches?

Avalanches can do a lot of damage. The power of an avalanche can destroy a whole town. The wind made by an avalanche can also be dangerous. The falling snow pushes the air in front of the avalanche at very high speeds. In 1962 an avalanche in Switzerland produced winds that snapped trees in half!

Sometimes an avalanche makes a wind that blows up more snow.

The effects of an avalanche can be seen for a long time after the snow stops moving. That's because an avalanche changes the land around it. Avalanches carry huge amounts of dirt from one area to another. One avalanche can move as much dirt as a river will move in one year!

This avalanche carried away so much dirt and snow, it left a path.

Can People Stop Avalanches?

Avalanches are a part of nature. There is no way to stop them from happening. However, people have learned ways to slow down the moving snow. Many people build fences or walls on the sides of mountains. People also plant trees as a natural wall to stop the snow. In some areas, people even make paths for the snow to follow! These paths lead the snow away from roads and towns.

These trees are slowing down some fast-moving snow.

In some mountain areas, people have built **snowsheds** to lead the snow away from the roads. A snowshed looks like a slanted roof over the road. When an avalanche hits the snowshed, the snow flies through the air and lands on the other side of the road!

Snowsheds like this one protect roads from dangerous avalanches.

Some scientists start avalanches on purpose. By starting smaller avalanches, scientists can clear away the heavy snow before a larger avalanche has a chance to start.

To start an avalanche, scientists find a patch of heavy snow that is hanging over the edge of a steep cliff. Then they clear all of the roads and surrounding areas of people. Finally, they use a large cannon to send explosives into the snow. The blast shakes the snow and starts a small avalanche.

This explosion was set off by scientists to start an avalanche.

How Can You Protect Yourself?

If you spend time in the mountains, it is important to be prepared. Before going hiking or skiing, make sure that you have the right equipment. When you are traveling on mountain slopes, always stay with a group. Most importantly, never go into unmarked or dangerous areas. Avalanches can happen without warning, so it is very important to stay in safe areas.

Many dangerous mountain areas have signs that warn people of avalanches.

So the next time you are in a snowy mountain area, look around. Can you see any drifts of snow hanging over a cliff? Are there any signs warning people to stay out of certain places? If there are, make sure to follow directions and stay safe. If you do, then you can enjoy the snowy outdoors without worrying about the avalanche!

This snowy mountain is another perfect place for an avalanche.

GLOSSARY:

dry snow avalanche (DRY SNOH AV–uh–lanch)
Dry snow avalanches happen when fine, powdery snow falls down a mountain.

slab avalanche (SLAB AV–uh–lanch)
Slab avalanches happen when huge chunks of snow fall down a mountain.

snowshed (SNOH–shed)
A snowshed is a roof that is built over a mountain road. When an avalanche hits a snowshed, the snow is sent flying to the other side of the road.

vibration (vy–BRAY–shun)
A vibration is a very small movement. Even a small vibration can cause an avalanche.

Index